CW01262978

Barrowford
in old picture postcards

by Peter Wightman

European Library ZALTBOMMEL/THE NETHERLANDS

BACK IN TIME

GB ISBN 90 288 6439 3

© 1997 European Library – Zaltbommel/The Netherlands

No part of this book may be reproduced in any form, by print, photoprint, microfilm or any other means, without written permission from the publisher.

Introduction

The following short chronology of Barrowford between the years 1880 and 1930 covers a similar period to that during which the postcards and other illustrations in this book were issued. It is intended as a guide to the background of a period that is just a little beyond the edge of our memories.

1880   Congregationalist chapel built.
       Independent Methodist chapel erected.
1881   Major storm causes severe flooding.
       Population of Barrowford 3,842.
1882   Blacko Tower commenced.
       3'10" dog otter caught at Newbridge.
1883   Chancel added to St. Thomas' Church.
       Assistant teacher at Blacko salary £40 per year.
1884   Thomas Edward Every Clayton (born in 1841) dies.
       200 members of Funeral Club hold annual tea party.
1885   Barrowcloughs reduce weavers' wages by 5%.
       Only 670 names on Barrowford voters list.
1886   Service reservoir at Pasture Head agreed.
       Methodists go in wagonettes to Buck Inn at Malham.
1887   Newbridge Co-op premises built.
       Water supply piped from Watermeetings.
1888   Railway proposed through Barrowford.
       Thomas Grimshaw (born in 1838) dies.
1889   Barrowford Almanac first issued.
       Lower Clough Mill built.
1890   Blacko Board School opened.
       First annual cycle race from Settle.
1891   School Board inaugurates free education.
       Amalgamation with Nelson scheme rejected.
1892   Newbridge Primitive Methodist Chapel opened.
       Treasurer of Progressive Co-op has deficiencies.
1893   Measles epidemic.
       Mill stoppages due to coal trade dispute.
1894   Temperance demonstrations.
       New Board school proposed.
1895   Daniel Nutter the butcher dies.
       Higherford: Wiseman's Mill strike settled.
1896   New Board school opened.
       Berry & Sons short time working.
1897   Building start of new police station.
       New Catholic church and school opened.
1898   Blacko: weavers' dispute.
       Co-operative Society Funds deficient.
1899   Gisburn Road Co-op premises purchased.
       Nuisance inspector appointed at £52 per annum.
1900   Catholic cemetery chapel foundation stone laid.
       Rates 2s.2d. in the £.
1901   Tramways proposed.
       Blacko: Trafford's Mill dispute and fire.
1902   Woman's sixth marriage service disrupted.
       Work begun on tram tracks.
1903   Albert Mills and Duckworth & Atkinson strikes.
       Tram service begins.
1904   Cycling invention by Tom Lowcock and Tom Grave.
       Lower Clough Mill extension.
1905   Newbridge Primitive Methodist School extension.
       Rev. E. Gough publishes a volume of verse.
1906   Bridge at Newbridge widened.
       Congregational Church diamond jubilee.
1907   Liberal Club closes and is sold.
       Lower Clough Mill strike.

1908	Barrowford Angling Association formed.
	Homefield Mill working commences.
1909	St. Thomas' burial ground extension proposed.
	Albert Mills strike.
1910	New Co-op premises opened.
	Caster Gill Clough bridge opened at Blacko.
1911	Church Street paved.
	Tom Grave becomes an aviator.
1912	Local Government inquiry into Gisburn Road.
	Nelson Girls' Friendly Society branch formed.
1913	Barrowford Brass Band formed.
	Diphtheria outbreak at Blacko.
1914	Cotton trade bad.
	Pte. W. Ashworth: an early one of many war deaths.
1915	Cotton trade picks up.
	Hargreaves found guilty of murder but insane.
1916	Pte. A. Shea, East Lancs. Reg. gets D.C.M. & M.M.
	2nd. Lieut. E. A. Holden death.
1917	Springfield Mill, Blacko, vandalised.
	Sutcliffe patent for producing manure from sewage.
1918	Blacko: Ebenezer Chapel jubilee.
	Mr. and Mrs. S. Holden provide Y.M.C.A. hut.
1919	Pte. Trew arwarded Croix de Guerre.
	Pte. F. Dewhurst awarded Mons Star.
1920	Barrowford Show has first band contest.
	Fred Bannister appointed headmaster.
1921	Birth rate 22.7 and death rate 12.7 per 1000.
	John Clegg, Blacko headmaster, retires.
1922	Higherford Mill re-starts after 14 months.
	Spiritualist Church to be formed in Back Lee Street.
1923	Blacko recreation ground opened.
	Council clerk resigns: blinded by assault.
1924	Dicky Nook demolished.
	Council receives title deeds to Park.
1925	Rates 11s.10d. in £.
	Library opens with 360 books.
1926	Gaumless Trough water ceases to flow.
	8,545 looms operating.
1927	Manchester & County Bank newly open.
	Fanny Stephenson; early woman preacher.
1928	St. Thomas' Church jubilee.
	A. Ridehalgh's book of short stories.
1929	'Annals & Stories of Barrowford' published.
	T. Ridehalgh of Blacko chairs Burnley R.D.C.

The sequence of illustrations in the main follows the river, going upstream from the Newbridge / Carr Hall area to the countryside at Blacko with occasional diversions.

Acknowledgement for detailed information and assistance is made to Mrs. Crowther of Beanfield House, to John Miller at Pendle Heritage Centre, to Susan Byrne at Nelson Library, Christine Ashworth and Sheila Cutler at Barrowford Library, to Tony Harulow at Blacko, and to the Fotofast family at Colne.

1 **Carr Hall.** Once a family residence of the Towneley family, the hall came into the Clayton family when Margaret Towneley married John Clayton in 1754. Later in the early nineteenth century Edward Every, after obtaining royal permission, became the first of the Every-Claytons. He lived at Carr Hall until his son Thomas Edward Every-Clayton (born in 1841) reached the age of 21. Thomas lived at Carr Hall untill he died in 1886 at the age of 45. Little seen outside his own estate he was of a retiring disposition. It was he who attemped to close down Carr Hall Road. On his death his son Henry took possession of the hall but he died in 1887. Edward, his younger brother, took possession of the property until Mr. Hezekiah Fletcher was announced in 1892 as being the new tenant. Edward Every-Clayton sold the estate to William Tunstill and his son H. Tunstill sold it to William Hartley, whose widow occupied it till her death in 1927. The hall, originally built about 1580, was demolished in 1954.

2 **Top Lodge, Carr Hall Road.** In 1907 inhabitants of the Carr Hall District expressed a desire to have a policeman stationed in the district to counter the lawless and disgraceful conduct of the rowdy element not residing there. Carr Hall Road in 1907 had houses numbered from 2 to 30 with resident families of Gill, Greenwood, Ramsden, Houldsworth, Slater, Whittam, Riley, Hartley, Holt, Rycroft, Speak, Holgate, Leeper and Landless. Boltons lived at Chestnut Cottage and Clements at Rose Hill. Mr. Halsall owned a piece of land used as a tennis court and Mr. Heap owned the land on which stood Carr Mill. By the following year additional houses had been built with Runnymede, Elsinore, Forest Banks and Applegarth bringing additional families of Watson, Robinson, Parker and another Hartley as well as a nice variety of additional house names. Perhaps the policeman had also brought a sobriety to this area of Newbridge Ward.

3   **Right of way, Carr Hall Road.** In the 1860s access along Carr Hall Road was allowed by Colonel Clayton of Carr Hall so that the public could more easily attend the Barley and Roughlee Anniversary services, with announcements being made from the appropriate Wesleyan pulpits. Disputes, however, arose, some members of the public intimating that they had an established right of way, Colonel Clayton saying that a disorderly element from Nelson were abusing their privilege. The case was tried at Colne – without a verdict – and at Liverpool where James Emmott was found guilty of breaking fences and damaging gates. In 1891 Edward Every-Clayton agreed with the Nelson Corporation to allow access on foot as a pleasure walk for a rent of £12, the Council to erect turnstiles at each end, to provide an iron fence where the road was unfenced, and to provide four field gates and wheeled traffic to be by permission of the owner only.

4 **Park Avenue.** In 1896 the plot of land upon which these houses were built was leased by John Haytock from the trustees of T.E.E. Clayton. The houses were numbered 2 to 10 Park Avenue from the right and around the corner to the left 2 to 24 Carr Hall Road. The same houses in Park Avenue today are numbered 34 to 42. John Haytock lived at 10 Park Avenue for many years, followed by Mrs. S. Wilmore. No. 8 belonged to Mr. T. Brandwood, the textile manager. Fred Greenwood, the schoolmaster, lived at 6, Annie Sagar at 4 and Mrs. Findley at number 2. Carr Hall Road had a Mr. James Gill at No. 2 for well over forty years from 1905, whilst the Houldsworth family further up at No. 10 were there from 1902 for fifty years. Horsfalls at 4 and Prestons at 12 were there from the 1920s for over 25 years; Steers at 18 and Parkers at 20 for over twenty years from the 1920s. There are tales to tell about all of them, perhaps some other time.

5 The Laund about 1910.

James Hargreaves was the last member of a family that had owned The Laund for several hundred years. He was a bachelor and lived the life of a country gentleman in this large fine establishment. He was also a solicitor but had never found it necessary to practise, and was not averse to using his powerful physique. Sarah Jane Haythornthwaite became his housekeeper for £20 a year in 1905. Sarah was pulled off the chair by the hair, pummelled with his fists and had her head violently knocked against the wall. The judge said he was quite out of his mind and the jury awarded £400 damages. Another housekeeper, Henrietta Appleyard, got £100 damages in 1914, and the 19-year old Frank Hinchcliffe who served a writ on him got shot in the back and died later. James was given a life sentence, died in Broadmoor in 1936, was buried in St. Thomas' churchyard at Barrowford and left £50,000 to Nelson Corporation.

6 **Reedyford Bar.** There were four bars encircling Barrowford and Blacko on the turnpike road: Blacko bar at the bend of the road above Blacko in the direction of Gisburn; another at the top of Reedyford brow; and two gates near the George and Dragon, one barring the way to Higherford, the other barring the way to Colne. Tolls were not charged for vehicles carrying the mails, nor for persons going to church, nor for the horses of soldiers, but cattle were charged at 1s. 3d. for twenty and sheep 7$^1/_2$d. for twenty. Horse-drawn vehicles paid from 4d. to 4 shillings with prices doubling on Sundays. John Porter attended the Reedyford bar, John West those at Barrowford, and families of Bullock and Walmsley that at Blacko. The toll bar system ceased to operate at midnight on the last day of June 1872, the Reedyford toll house was sold to a Mr. Tunstill for £40, and the Turnpike Trust ceased on 1st November 1872.

7 Newbridge and the river.

Barrowford has an affinity for floods with major problems regularly occurring at Newbridge. 5th July 1881 is a renowned date when between 10 p.m. and 11 p.m. the village witnessed a lightning pyrotechnic display of terrific splendour and torrential rain. Gisburn Road became a vast rushing river, Newbridge was converted into a lake, hen pens with their livestock were borne downstream and carried away. The morning after, the road was a rubbish tip of sand and stones. There were timber pieces that the previous day were bridges upstream together with pieces of furniture recognised as coming from Barley. The floods continued in 1901, 1903, 1911, 1920 and 1926. In 1928 the council appointed a special committee to prevent a recurrence and spent £170 in March 1935 to take out big stones and boulders from the river. In 1996 a new £7.5 million scheme was announced to solve the problem.

8 **Newbridge.** In 1891 not all the residents of Newbridge wanted to be part of Barrowford and proposed that with Carr Hall estate they should become part of Nelson and gain a reduction of 3d. per 1,000 feet in the supply of gas. When Newbridge comprised only a score of houses, eight of them were on the Nelson side of the river. Newbridge also had a total of 4,000 looms while the total for all other parts of Barrowford was only 3,492. On the right of the picture Edgar Dean's pie and pea shop was next to the pub. Usually you would find fifteen folk there eating hot home-made pies with lashings of salt and vinegar on the peas; digestion invigorated with locally-made fizzy pop in marble stoppered bottles; open all day and night till 9 p.m.; the whole to be capped by a visit to the pub afterwards. What a gay life! Then there was the confectioners where Sam Holden's staff went for lunch; and a selling-out shop at the end of Lee Street.

9 Newbridge Methodists.

With the development of the cotton industry the Newbridge end of Barrowford became a centre of building activity and saw large increases in population. The Primitive Methodist part of that population met in the Co-op Assembly Rooms but became inconveniently crowded with eighty scholars and fifty adults. A new building was therefore proposed that could accommodate 250 people in three vestries and the site could later take a sizeable chapel. It was hoped to help young people 'out of vice and all the multitudinous seductions of the present time' and as treasurer they appointed Jesse Blakey. It was built in 1892 at a cost of £1,398 and in 1904 two further vestries were added to cope with the 106 boys and 89 girls who needed to be 'trained in the principles of righteousness'. Unfortunately the movement never witnessed the prosperity it might have expected and the reason remains a mystery.

10 **Police station.** The photograph shows police sergeant and constable with their wives about 1900. All had living accommodation on the premises. Also evident is the very early police pillar that provided a telephone link to the police station when the latter was closed. The 1933 Barrett's directory lists John Hopper as police sergeant and Ronald Almond as police constable. A hundred years earlier in the mid-1840s two other policemen had clashed with a group of half a dozen bruisers turned out of the Fleece Inn sometime after midnight. They were seen with wooden staves in a thick mist. The morning after there were pools of blood spattered over the whole area after two constables had received a terrible battering, with one of them never recovering. None of the assailants were ever apprehended for lack of evidence. A lot of people knew the perpetrators, yet no one divulged the incriminating knowledge of their neighbours.

11 **Tramways.** In 1901 Barrowford Council decided to be up to date and have tramways, with a Mr. Fraser, electrical engineer, to have 3% of the capital expenditure. Later it was agreed that the 'light railway' be run as a joint venture with Nelson, Barrowford paying 2d. per unit for all current used. During the excavations in 1903, 130 men were working on the project with only one mishap, when a horse and landau ended up in the bottom of one of the road holes. The entire works were carried out in two months. In 1907 the Rev. A. F. Studdy, preaching in St. Thomas' Church, said the Sunday tram business was an evil, it had destroyed the peace of the day, and urged the Council to follow Southport by banning the vehicles on Sunday. Behind the police station on the right was a garage owned by a Cuthbert Berry, who enjoyed the taste of alcohol. His family owned Victoria Mill, their house being across the road on the left.

12 **The Boltons.** In 1896 John Bolton had established a business as a painter at 68 Gisburn Road. By 1905 he described himself additionally as a paper hanger, sign writer and decorator, with other premises at Nelson. By 1918 a Miss Clara Bolton had a shop next door at Number 70 and by 1923 a Clement Bolton had appeared at 66. He was also a painter and at 68 in 1924. In 1927 Clement had a house at 66 with the John Bolton firm given as at 66-68. The business in Nelson at 79a Scotland Road was still going well and included an agency for enamel and copper lettering. By 1937, however, a weaver named F. Rawson lived at 66, a Miss J. Carman was a hairdresser at 68, Clara Bolton was still a grocer at 70, but the John Bolton had left Nelson. Today you can see the door numbers with some difficulty and the heavy green paintwork incongruously displays a rusting bus stop sign. It is unlikely that John Bolton would be impressed with its present state of decoration.

13 **Weavers' cottages.** The architectural charm of Barrowford is superbly captured in John Miller's 'Walk through Barrowford', published in May 1973. These weavers' cottages numbered 78 to 86 in Gisburn Road had stone hoods over the doors and elongated chimney pieces, the stone materials for their construction very likely being brought from a convenient local quarry. The occupancy of the cottages can be determined by use of the local directories and the Register of Electors for Barrowford, the latter being available on microfilm at Nelson Library covering the period 1872-1938. In the 1890s number 78 was occupied by Robert Hargreaves until the arrival of Aaron Oldfield in 1899; R. Corless, weaver, was there in 1937 and A. Simpson, labourer, in 1941 and 1949. Number 80 was occupied by James Watson until the arrival of William Blair in 1893; H. Kimberley, taper, was there from 1937 to 1945 and a B. Waddington in 1949.

14 **Council School** about 1920. Lady O'Hagan opened the school on 25th March 1897. It replaced rented facilities for infants in the Primitive Methodist School (the tall building behind is the Primitive Methodist Church) and facilities for older children at the Congregationalists. The School Board had provided a 5,961 sq.yds. site for 320 infants and 510 older ones with 60-80 scholars in each of the eleven classrooms that had access to a large central hall accommodating 1,000. Mr. Webber was the first headmaster and served 42 years before his retirement in 1920. He died at his house in Rushton Street in 1947 at the age of 94. Fred Bannister, a native of Trawden, was the second headmaster and began with a salary of £450 per year in 1921 at the age of 44. He worked in a cotton factory from the age of 10 until he was 19, later getting two university degrees. His 100-page 'Annals of Trawden Forest' was published in 1922 at 6d. a copy.

15 **May Day,** 1923. The third year of celebrations organised by the local school. All pupils had a voice as to who should be the May Queen and all the girls made their own dresses. The weekend event had dancing all day, three-legged races, with tea and buns for everybody afterwards. The first May Queen was Annie Blacka, whose mace bearer Gogo Jackson didn't like it as he felt he was being made to look like a sissy. Another May Queen was Mary Nutter, who lived at Parkhill with her father James 'Wiggy' (wore a wig) Holden. The group shown here are, from left to right, back row: Nancy Cronshaw, Doris Skinner, Gertie Seed, Irene Sharp, Ethel Charles and Dorothy Binns. Middle row: Edwin Dyson, Nellie Potter, Margaret Burrows, Jessie Metcalfe, Olive Stansfield (May Queen), Linda Driver, Nora Woods and Ethel Walker. Front row, Robert Livock, ?, Alfred Roberts, Mary Higgins and Ernest Duerden.

16 **Gaumless.** For over a hundred years water flowed from 30 feet below ground level at West Hill to this trough that once stood beside Gisburn Road in the area of the present Fountain Street flats. Henry Armistead sank the well; a legal document of 1847 records the other 22 with whom he shared it. Scores of times it stopped, but the natives looked on it as an old friend. The trough was replaced by a Gaumless Fountain in 1911, a luxury version with separate basins for dogs, horses and humans. The Barnoldswick carrier's horse could not pass without a drink and made that extra effort as it approached. Nature's valuable beverage was said to contain iron, smell not very pleasant, taste not much better, make splendid tea but to have limited uses in washing clothes. Moved to the cemetery in the early 1960s it has ceased to be the antidote to sciatica, rheumatism, gout, distemper, rabies, obesity, colic and 'bowels'.

17　**Water Street.** Not the pleasantest place to live, but most of us cannot choose where we are born or often where we live and work. Numbers 1 to 7 and 2 to 10 were the few houses in Water Street that housed a good proportion of weavers within their walls. Much of the tightly-packed housing had been 'designed' to cope with the influx of mill operatives attracted by the boom in the textile manufacturing trade. In the background is the Congregational Church, its views of heaven overlooking the stark reality of everyday living. The Congregationalists had their early meetings in Mrs. Baldwin's warehouse and the Temperance Hall in Pasture Lane, the instrumental accompaniment being provided by Robert Leeming's bass fiddle. The church in the picture was built in 1881 and demolished in 1976, a former minister, Rev. T. A. Nicholson, preaching the final sermon on 25th January 1976.

18 **The Dandy Shop.** These cottages in Water Street were erected in 1851, the top floor probably being used, as in many other three-floored houses, for hand loom weaving. The outside staircase would allow weavers a measure of privacy for domestic affairs. It is suggested that they were known as dandy shops due to the fact that the new light weight iron looms installed were far more convenient (dandy) than the earlier heavy wooden ones. 10 Water Street and the two cottages next door at the time formed the Liberal Club, where mill tea parties were held with dancing to piano, concertina and fiddle; the men dressed in stiff collars and shirt fronts, the ladies in long dresses that only occasionally came above the ankle. In 1907 Jonas Brown converted the Club into three separate buildings, Mr. and Mrs. Kaylow being in No. 10 until 1958, raising nine children and paying from 3s9d. to 8s.6d. a week in rent during the tenancy.

19 **King's Mill.** It has been suggested that the original mill on this site may have been one of the ancient fulling mills which were introduced into this locality as early as 1311. More certain is that a Robert Bannister of Colne Hall left it in 1781 to his trustees, who sold it as a cloth or fulling mill to Christopher and Abraham Hargreaves for £233. Subsequent lessees of the mill include William Brightmore, John Hudson, Henry Armistead, John Tunstill and a John Fell. In 1924 the Council bought the old mill, cottages and gardens, reservoir, goit and canal for £1,000. In July 1932 the Nelson Leader noted that 'another landmark in the village is now being destroyed in the demolition of the Old Mill' and that a Mrs. Elliott had generously provided for swings and other amenities. The present playground now occupies its site and all that remains is the ruined angle of a building embedded in this hillside of the park.

The King's or "Carre Mill," Nelson.

20 **Totty.** Totty is a name that does not often appear in this area. Its meaning indicates a tiny tot, unsteady, shaky, dizzy, dazed, tipsy or fuddled, and was used as early as 1386. A considerable number of Tottys are recorded in the Leeds, Bradford and Wakefield areas of Yorkshire. The name is mentioned in the Nelson Rate Books of 1845 onwards where James, John and Robert Totty were at Woverdale and Scholefield farms. There was a John Tottie, butcher in Barrowford in 1879, but most well known was the shop at 103 Gisburn Road, where John Totty had his business from 1896 until the mid thirties, when J. S. Rushford in 1937 and in 1949 Green & Son carried on the butchery trade. There were of course other Tottys: Ellen Alice of 1 Bankhouse Street who died in 1933 aged 47; Wilson Totty, a coachman, of 205 Gisburn Road in 1923; James Totty, who lived at Blacko until his death in 1944, came from a well known Barrowford family.

21 **Nrs. 105 - 123 Gisburn Road about 1920.** These are the buildings on the right of the picture: 105, whose tall side only can be seen to the centre left of the picture, housed Stephen Harper, a bootmaker and grocer in 1890, Henry Holden, tripe dresser, in 1896 and from 1899 Henry Lee in the same trade. H. Astin used it for a restaurant in the 1920s before reverting to the trade in tripe. The smaller building near us with a poster on the bottom left was 107, where Tom Lowcock was a boot, shoe and clog maker; in 1899 Samuel Jackson was a blacksmith, machinist and cycle dealer, and in the 1920s and 1930s H. Wood used the premises as an antique dealer. 109 was Buckle's shop from 1890 onwards and Harold Dixon used 111 as a fruiterers from 1914. Numbers 109-113 were demolished in the 1930s for road widening. 115, Eastham's house, was demolished about 1936 and 117 onwards became Barrowford Co-op. The buildings on this side of the steps were the Fleece Inn.

22 **Shopping centre.** On the left of the picture is the road that led up to the Lamb Club. The Co-op is the building with the blinds outside. Near is the greengrocers shop run by Betsy Buckle that later became Harold Dixons. At the time of the photograph few children had many sweets but spent their pocket money on carrots and turnips. To the right of the van was Miss Rule's shop – a confectionery business with the house and bakery on the same premises. Wesley Clegg was the main removal firm with little opposition in the area. John Totty's shop was off the left of the picture. The early Co-op, known as 'Th' Union', was first in The Square before removing to opposite the Gaumless trough in 1847 and in 1852 to Sutcliffe's buildings. Initially open at night for distributive purposes, in 1853 it was open all day. The first committee members met in the store room and discussed developments whilst sitting on sacks of flour.

23 **Two wheelers.** John Hargreaves, a one-legged cyclist active from the 1890s, described cycling as glorious and exhilarating. In his first road race he came third and in the second – a race from Barrowford to Skipton and back – his opponent gave up half way. About 1920 he challenged another one-legged cyclist for the Championship of the North but nothing came of it. By trade he was an oat-cake baker carrying 40lbs. of cakes in a basket strapped to his back. Tom Lowcock was another famous local cyclist who began work as a boot, shoe and clog maker in 1893 at 107 Gisburn Road, acting also as cycle agent in 1896 when he had moved to 79a; a cycle repairer by 1899; a cycle maker in 1908 at 96 Gisburn Road. He had a vigorous constitution, was involved in the career of Tom Grave, patented a circumvolving loop and worked on an elliptical revolving wheel project. He died of rheumatic fever in 1910 leaving a family of ten children.

24 **Tom Grave.** An invention of an extraordinary nature for trick cycling was the invention of two Barrowford men, Tom Lowcock and Tom Grave. Within a huge wooden wheel that revolved at 20 m.p.h. Tom Grave would cycle at 60 m.p.h. in contrary motion to the wheel. After twelve months of training and trials at the Old Mill in Barrowford, there was a first public performance at the Empire Theatre, Burnley, in August 1904. The event was an immense success: the vast audience went wild, the stalls clapped, the pit shouted, the gods whistled and stamped to delirium. News of the act spread and performances followed all over the country, all over Europe and into South Africa, from where Tom and his brother James returned just before the 1914 war brought an end to the act that had from 1909 included a miniature car. Tom Grave's stage name was Darracq. A rival – Le Diablo – was summonsed in 1907 for patent infringement.

25 Nrs. 98 - 122 Gisburn Road in 1920s. This area today is a very busy area of Barrowford and was no less so when trams, bicycles and clogs held sway in contrast to the car, motorbike and trainers. The house with lace curtains is 122: occupied by James Singleton (1890), William Thomas Booth (1893), George Dobney (1899), all greengrocers; James Astin, confectioner (1924), J. Blemiar, florist (1941); and Miss B. Horsley, draper (1949). Several times 120 and 122 were run as one business: in 1893 William Booth used both, as did J. Astin in 1924 and Miss Horsley in 1949. The post office at 110 was run by Mrs. I. Johnson in 1945 and A. Dugdale in 1949. Previously it had been a boot and shoemakers and milliners (Jonas Sharp and Mrs. A. Sharp 1890-1941). Another long resident on the row was John Hargreaves: he was a weaver living there from 1902 until 1937. Only Mrs. Hargreaves was there in 1941 and in 1949 an L. Kitchen shared the residence – listed as a traveller.

26 **Sutcliffe building.** From 1853 Barrowford Industrial Co-operative Society occupied these premises until the new central stores were opened on the same site in 1910. Membership had only been twenty in 1850 but in 1900 the number was 390, with a turnover increased from £500 to £10,000. Sutcliffe Buildings, erected in the 18th century and initially occupied by the Bannister family, were bought by the Co-op in 1899 for £800, including land. In the ten years up to 1910 sales were £99,000 with dividend and interest £13,000. By 1915 sales were £14,000 a year and at the annual tea and concert, to which each Co-op member got one free ticket with the option of an extra one for 6d, 800 people turned up. In July 1921 staff wages were reduced by 15%, a strike followed and the threat of immediate replacement of employees was carried out. In 1932, after two years of negotiations, Barrowford Co-op merged with that of Nelson.

27 **Bank Hall about 1920.** The porch and wing of this impressive house, now known as the Lamb Working Men's Club, were built by Thomas and Grace Sutcliffe (Hartley) in 1696, possibly re-using material from an earlier part of the main building. Architecturally quite interesting it shows the preferred late seventeenth-century style of a three-cell frontage and a curious entry position related to the lobby entrance. The White Bear in Barrowford, Carrybridge Hall and Hobstones in Colne show similar features. Bank Hall has carved kneelers on the gable filials, chamfered mullioned windows, and ogee mouldings on the exterior mullions. The upper windows in the gables light a false attic. From Sutcliffes, the house passed to the Craggs, and in 1898 to John Strickland, who sold it for £587 to Edmondson Widdup, John Whipp and John Gabbatt of the Working Men's Institute.

28 **Glee Union.** Barrowford Glee Union used to meet in the Co-operative Rooms, Church Street, and has had a chequered career. In 1905 the Nelson Leader expressed sorrow that the choir had been disbanded: 'There were some very good voices connected with it and there was every prospect of the party excelling at the divine art.' Eight years later in May 1913 the newspaper announced that 'the village has lagged in the march of music but at last has shaken off its wonted lethargy and there now seems a prospect of regaining the musical position held by Barrowford a generation ago. We are now to have a Barrowford male voice choir with Mr. Roland Dixon as conductor'. The membership rose to sixty by 1914 and won some prizes in the 1930s. In 1961 Mr. Harry Dixon said: 'We have entered for the Nelson festival, but whether we get there is another question.' In November 1961 by 16 votes to 4 the choir once again ceased to function.

29 Invasion by Primitives.

Barrowford was missioned from Colne after John Wesley had been forced into the river by a mob led by the Rev. White from Colne. Near to the same spot came W. Hartley, a schoolmaster from Trawden, who was grandfather to Sir W. P. Hartley, the jam manufacturer and local benefactor. He preached the first sermon in front of the beer shop that later became the Co-op stores. In 1824 meetings were held in John Clark's cottage near the White Bear Inn, with services conducted by William Robinson and others from Barley. In 1834 a room was taken over the house of John Veevers at the top of Bank Stile. Services were held here for two years until the first chapel was opened in 1837 by a Mr. Butcher, who walked from Skipton and back to perform the ceremony. John Veevers' house is shown in this photograph that was taken in the 1920s. It had become 7 Church Street and was demolished in the winter of 1958/9.

30 **Primitive Methodist Chapel, Church Street.** The first chapel of the Primitives was opened in 1837 after considerable efforts by voluntary workers, including the minister who helped to dig the foundations. However, this first chapel proved too small and the one pictured here was built just across the road and officially opened in 1873. The first attempt at construction was a disaster – it had to be demolished and a fresh start made that added £700 to the total cost. The Rev. Travis was in the circuit from 1884 until 1887 on a salary of 12s. a week and of that he spent 10s. on board and lodgings with a deduction of 6d. for each time he had his tea elsewhere. By 1895 all debts were cleared and new money spent on an organ that was opened by the international figure of W. H. Jude in 1896. In 1926 electric light was installed at a cost of £85. In March 1962 Arnolds Electronics were installed and used the building to overhaul refrigerators and washing machines.

31 **Barrowford Church.** The cornerstone of the church was laid in 1837, the church opened in 1841, enlarged in 1855, and the chancel added in 1882/3. When first opened the Wesleyan Choir assisted with the singing. In 1882, upon the installation of a new £400 organ, the old one was given to the Primitive Methodists. A church reunion in February 1928 was said to have produced one of the greatest social events in local history – 400 people attended the opening tea. Evening celebrations centred in the Council School. After musical 'renderings' of 'In an old fashioned town', 'Love's old sweet song', and 'O God our help in ages past' reminiscences followed. One was of Thomas Brookes, the church schoolmaster who knew how to use the stick; the lad who was sent to cut the stick from a neighbouring tree invariably being the first to feel it. Up to its centenary in 1941 there had been 867 marriages, 2,947 baptisms and 3,667 funerals.

32 **Oaklands** was built in 1860 by John Barrowclough, the principal cotton manufacturer and spinner in Barrowford. His grandson John sold it to James Ridehalgh (JP) in 1906. His son James Ridehalgh married Elizabeth Lonsdale. John, their son, ran Higherford Mill and lives at Blacko; another son Harold owns Burnt House Farm near Crossgaits, and their daughter Elizabeth became an estate agent at Grindleton. James' (JP) other son Arthur became a barrister in the West Indies and a judge in the Gold Coast. James (JP) died in 1936 at the age of 69 having spent most of his working life as a cotton manufacturer at Edward Street and later Lowerclough Mill. His wife died in 1941 at the age of 74. Before marriage she was a Miss Feather, her brother being the cemetery superintendent at Nelson. Oaklands was sold in 1941 for £6,550, becoming the N.F.S. headquarters for billets with office work carried out at night in the stables.

33 **Clough Farm.** William Sutcliffe (68) and his wife Sarah (64) occupied Clough Farm in 1881, employing two men on their 38 acres. One was their son Hartley (25), the other a Mitchell Dewhirst (25) from Kildwick, who boarded with them. In 1891 Hartley Sutcliffe, now 35, and his wife Mary (36) lived there with their sons Ben (5), a scholar, and James (3). The land, farm, garden, orchard, barn, mistal and stables came into the ownership of John Holt of Parkhill in 1891. After the death of John and his wife Anne in 1920 the farm was purchased in 1921 by James Ridehalgh. After his death in 1936 his executors let Clough Farm in 1930 to Arthur Lawson Dean, from whom it was transferred to Barrowford Council in 1951. In 1974 the Council sold for £3,750 a plot of land from Clough Farm to the charitable organisation named 'Help the Aged' and on that land was built the sheltered housing now known as St. Clement's Court.

34 **Vinegar Works** (Spring Clough Brewery). Three times a brewery and once a corn mill, the premises have been in the hands of several owners. First of them was Hartley and Bell, followed by a John Kenyon, who would travel from Rossendale to visit his works every Thursday and be collected by a Jonas Brown and trap at Nelson station. Jonas, born at Earby, was in charge of the brewery, ruling with a stern but kindly hand until his death in 1910 aged 73. Beer was free to employees and to passers-by who accepted invitations to sample the brew. In 1934 the mill was sold to Arthur Dean, proprietor of Nelson Corn Mills, with premises at Higherford. Later it became part of Massey's Burnley Brewery, then was named Burnley Clubs Brewery, then Lancashire Clubs Brewery with, in 1949, a £100,000 plan to produce 1,000 barrels a week in a scheme where clubs would get a bonus of fifty shillings for each barrel sold. In 1960 it became Gibbs Keg Brewery Ltd.

35 **The Grove.** Known originally as The Parsonage, this building was home to the first vicar of St. Thomas', Barrowford, the Rev. Samuel Smith, who lived there with his two maiden sisters-in-law, Elizabeth Amabell Brooks and Anna Maria Brooks, both of whom were born in India, lived on annuities and objected to school children having curls or having roses in their hats. He was a widower with one daughter, Frances Amabell, who was born in Barrowford, whilst he came from Epsom. In the 1920s it was Dr. Watson's Nursing Home. In 1943 it became a 24-hours war-time nursery to cope with children up to five years whose mothers were at work. In 1949 it was a relief hospital but was closed in 1975 due to a decrease in the number of patients, down from an average of 29 to one of 15. Later used as a centre for mentally handicapped children, it was declared surplus to requirements in 1983 and is now Belgarth Nursing Home.

36 **Wheatley Lane Inghamite Chapel.** Disposal of corpses has always been a problem unless of course you happened to be four-legged or had feathers. Then you would be slaughtered and dismembered in the prime of life and be eaten without a second thought. However, when the human population of this area was expanding at such a tremendous rate the usual churchyards could not cope and additional accommodation was required for the lifeless homes of the chromosomes. Cemeteries had to be opened at Colne (1860), Nelson (1894), the Catholic cemetery at Wheatley Lane (1900) and Barrowford (1930). The monumental inscriptions for Higherford Methodist Church date from 1834, St. Thomas' Church Barrowford start in 1839, but those at Wheatley Lane Inghamite Chapel are from 1750. Only just over the Barrowford boundary, it is still a very popular place, having been extended recently by the purchase of two additional acres of land.

Inghamite Chapel, Wheatley Lane.

37 **View over the park.** The road to Gisburn goes from left to right across the picture. The building centre left is the Lamb Club (Bank Hall), built by Thomas and Grace Sutcliffe in 1696; the vicarage, somewhat higher, was built in 1879 at a cost of £2,300. The vicars were Samuel Smith 1842-1877, A.F.S. Studdy 1877-1913, F.W. Fairhurst 1913-1934 and H. C. Hill 1934-1942. Oaklands in the distance was owned by James Hayhurst, the chemist, in 1946 and was sold to the MacAdam family about 1956. The two MacAdam sons were self-employed car repairers. Albert Mills on the right of the picture were built at the time of the Crimean War for mule spinning, but the equipment was later replaced by looms. Numerous firms have occupied the spacious premises besides the Barrowcloughs 1851-. These include: James Aitken 1891; Robert Cook 1902; Sunfield manufacturing Co. 1902-1923; Riley, Nuttal & Co. Ltd. 1923-1933.

38 **White Bear Inn.** Probably so called on account of the reputed bull and bear baiting that took place at its front, where originally there was a semi-circular wall with foundations three feet thick – similar to the 2ft. 6 in. walls of the building front. Formerly known as Hargreaves Great House it was built in 1667 by a James Hargreaves. In the Barrowford survey of 1903 Abraham Hargreaves is given as the owner of Charles Farm, public house and brew house, Charles Farm being occupied by a John Bracewell. Following other members of her family, Betsy Midgeley was the victualler at the turn of the century, whilst James Ridehalgh looked after the White Bear farm. The victualler in 1908 was James Almond, in 1911 Benjamin Taylor, in 1923 W. Shorrocks, in 1933 A. Clarkson, and in the 1940s J. Frankland. The impact of the White Bear on the area is much diminished by the monster of Albert Mills in its background.

39 **Snow Scene.** Hargreaves and Haworth, ironmongers and newsagents, had a shop on the right from about 1905 until 1937. Robinson Hargreaves was also a councillor for Barrowford specialising in education, and a member of the Primitive Methodists. He took the shop over from Jesse Blakey after 1902. Robinson Hargreaves' father was James Hargreaves, who built 1-11 Ford Street and also the Wesleyan Chapel at Barley. Later part of the shop block became Barrowcloughs – stationers in 1914, music instrument dealers in 1933 and radio dealers in 1937. Speaks newsagents were there in the 1940s. Across the road on the left was the doctors' surgery. First there was Dr. F. de Beeho Pim, then Dr. Sellars, then Dr. Chevassut. Part of the building was council offices. In the next block was J. H. Foulds, the butcher, who lived at Blacko. Next on the left was another butcher's shop, Burrows.

AI ROWFORD IN A SNOWSTORM.   HARGREAVES & HOWARTH, STATIONERS, BARROWFORD

42 **Local Board.** Members and officials of the first Barrowford Local Board in 1892 are, from left to right, back row: J. C. Waddington (clerk), James Dugdale, R. H. Wiseman, James Bracewell and Thomas Faraday. Second row: John Hartley, Daniel Nutter, James Baldwin, Martin England and Dr. Pim (medical officer). Front row: John Emmott, J. C. Howson (Craven Bank) and J. Whittingham (clerk to Mr. Waddington). Each one has his own story. Dr. F. E. de Beelio Pim took a great interest in the St. John Ambulance Brigade. In 1882 he was an instructor in bandaging in Dublin and four years later gave the first of his annual series of lectures in Barrowford. In 1919 he was appointed Assistant Commissioner, Lancashire, controlling 2,000 members of all ranks. On leaving Barrowford he lived at Eastfield, Nelson, where he continued as consulting physician and surgeon. He died in 1936 shortly after moving to Sidmouth.

43 Nrs. 134 and 136 Gisburn Road. The address of Jesse Blakey's shop from which business address he published the Barrowford Almanac from 1889. From its pages he quoted extensively in his later book 'The Annals and Stories of Barrowford', which when issued in 1929 cost six shillings, by post sixpence extra. In spite of it having absorbing interest and value – 'its perusal will bring laughter and tears to those in far flung fields of the British Empire' – Mr. Blakey was quite expecting a serious loss in connection with the book. Jesse was, however, a prosperous businessman, of fine physique, common sense and sterling character. A Primitive Methodist, he had two sons, lived at Hibson Road, Nelson, and was a Nelson town councillor. At his silver wedding celebrations in December 1908 he was entertained at the Primitive Methodist School by the 'wonderful whistling productions' of Mr. Harry Wellock. Those were the days!

44 **Halstead Lane.** The building on the left was a joiner's shop. The cart is decorated for a procession walk that would normally end up in Barrowford Park. The cart belonged to Hargreaves and Son, coal merchants, and was borrowed to show a green-grocery display. The Hargreaves lived down Newbridge. Newbridge, Barrowford and Higherford were three separate places, each community keeping to themselves. Most of the area's children, however, went to Rushton Street School, whose head was a Mr. Webber, who also lived in Rushton Street. Fred Bannister then came as head. He always wore his M. A. cap and gown. Both his two daughters became teachers. Another teacher at Barrowford was a Miss Kirkpatrick, who hailed from Ireland. She used a thumb operated 'click click' signal device as an aid to teaching. Women teachers always wore long dresses down to the ankles. Such was Miss Armitage who did all the caning.

45 **Pasture House.** Pasture House at the top of Halstead Lane is mentioned in the early Colne Parish Church registers: Lettice, daughter of Wm. Kenyon, was baptised on 12 February 1662; Josias, son of James Foulds, on 1 October 1752; Joseph Hellowell was buried on 28 November 1750 and James Smith on 10 May 1736. All of Pasture House. In the 1803 survey of Barrowford the rateable value of the house was given as £3.10.6 with James Walton the occupier. In 1829 it was leased to Ingham Walton by a John Mitchell of Halifax for £75 a year, this sum also including payment for various out buildings and parcels of land. This Ingham Walton married a Sarah Sutcliffe. Round the turn of the century John Foulds was farmer here; in 1914 Frank Smith, in 1923 Dan Carradice and in the 1930s and 1940s Nelson Co-op ran the farm with the District Council and Town Planning Officer allowing in 1945 the erection of a dairy subject to it receiving a coat of cement wash.

46 **Hartleys Garage.** Road improvements have deprived us of many interesting old buildings, this being one that until the early 1930s stood at the bottom of Halstead Lane. The left-hand building, 151 Gisburn Road, was occupied by the clogger Thomas Holt in 1890 and in 1911 by F.W.H. Streeting, a cycle dealer. George Hartley had appeared on the scene in 1914 and until the road widening he operated from there as a cycle agent and a motor engineer with additional premises at 213 Gisburn Road. Those latter premises are still in use for motors under the name of Quick Service Garage. George Hartley lived at 8 Westhill but later resided at 8 Bankhouse Street, Barrowford. Robert Foulds in 1896, and J.H. Foulds from 1911 were butchers next door at 153 Gisburn Road. 155 Gisburn Road used to be occupied by Mr. Welsh, a wood turner, but later became the premises of the Barrowford Horticultural and Allotments Society and Institute.

47 **Nrs. 191-211 Gisburn Road, 1920s.** When in 1908 it was decided to pave Gisburn Road from Newbridge to Higherford Bridge, the view was put forward that the houses on each side of the main street would be free from dust and dirt and that there would be heard much less of that language from cyclists and others which tended to shock the ears and minds of men and women of fine taste and moral culture. In 1923 attention was drawn to the fact that trams came so close to the kerbstones that no person could pass in safety, there was no pavement of any width to walk on, the road was positively dangerous and shopkeepers bitterly complained of mud-splashed windows. The application to replace trams with buses between Nelson centre and Higherford was made in November 1933 and granted by the Traffic Commissioners of the North West area. The first building on the right is William Whitaker's forge: 'Bill Blacksmith' operated there from 1912 until 1961.

48 **Stansfield Roberts.** Barrowford in Edwardian times had a curious mixture of trades and professions when viewed by today's standards. Robert Pate was an umbrella maker, Lizzie Simpson was a stocking knitter, Albert Slater was a yeast dealer, D. Metcalfe was a drainer, R. Sharples a horse slaughterer and James Gudgeon a cowkeeper. Richard Nowell was both a chemist and a dentist; Jesse Blakey an ironmonger and stationer. Stansfield Roberts of 21 Ford Street was a coal dealer and undertaker in 1908 with 'open and closed car hearse and best Clarence carriages. Also hearsettes for children's funerals. The only one in the district. Broughams for evening parties with foot warmers if required. Cabs and traps at any hour of the day or night'. His own funeral followed in August 1947 when he was 75 and his obituary recorded that Barrowford had lost one of its best known servants.

49 Outside the George and Dragon about 1880. The George and Dragon is on the left, Syke House in the centre. Behind the horse and cart is the toll house. The man with the tall hat is a Mr. Sagar and the other is Mr. Buckle. The late-Georgian style Syke House, built in 1822, was the home of Mary Walton, a straw bonnet maker in 1841; of Ignatius Walton, a druggist in 1851; of Isaac Henry Evans, a grocer in 1861; of Samuel Howarth, a retired confectioner in 1871; of John Hartley, a retired farmer in 1881, who lived there with his daughter Alice and two assistant teachers – Elizabeth Oakley and Lily Meredith. The George and Dragon victualler between 1897 and 1905 was a William Haworth, in 1914 John Harker, in the 1920s and 1930s Fortescue Hewitson, and J. Livesey Cook in the 1940s. In the 1960s the inn attempted to popularise a jazz club sideline under the landlord Jack Ashton, but its success was somewhat limited.

50 **Park Hill.** On the death of Parker Swinglehurst Holt in 1890, his brother John Holt acquired Park Hill. John died on 20th December 1920 and in 1924 Lower Park Hill farm was purchased by Samuel Holden, John Dixon and Barrowford U.D.C. for a park, Higher Park Hill being transferred to Hartley Sutcliffe in 1921. When James (Wiggy) Holden lived at Lower Park Hill there was a trout stream that could be approached through an archway, and local children had never seen such enormous quantities of apples and oranges that were stored in his kitchen area. He had three daughters: Eleanor (m. W.H. Nutter), Elizabeth (m. H. Thomas), and Mary (m. F.W. Burrows). When Albert Armistead from Brierfield became clerk to Barrowford Council, part of Lower Park Hill was altered into a residence for him. His family included twin boys: John became a surveyor at Colne and Jack became a bank manager there. Albert died in 1967.

51 **Barrowford Locks.**
Although actually in Colne, the area is more usually associated with Barrowford and it is from these seven locks that the level of this canal lowers by some 69 feet. Minor mishaps do occur, one such being that of the steamer 'Clyde', when about midday on Monday 4th October 1890, with a William Baldwin as captain, she was proceeding from Leeds to Liverpool with a cargo of farrago, she hit a wooden post protruding vertically from the bottom of the lock. The post entered the hull while she was descending in the lock and the steamer sank, but not being entirely submerged there was little damage to the cargo. By six she was mended, by seven she had sailed away. In the past the locks have been voted the best kept in the whole of Britain and on several occasions have received awards for being runners-up. A study published in 1972 suggested a picnic site just below the locks with barbecue and parking facilities.

52 Higherford Wesleyan Methodist Chapels in 1890s.

Methodism is known to have existed at Barrowford in 1779, one of its leaders being James Ridehalgh, a farmer from Parkhill, where preaching services were likely to have been held. A small group of them determined to build a chapel on land given by James Walton and on Whit Monday 1801 it was opened. Barrowford at that time had about 130 houses, 30 above the chapel and 100 below. Enlarged in 1813, with alterations in 1860 and 1879, the old chapel was converted into a Sunday School upon the opening of the new chapel in 1890 that would seat 650. In the earlier chapel four constables regularly attended and during the singing of the second hymn they would go out, scour the village for any loiterers and compel them either to go to chapel or go home. In 1962 the tower was reported to be unsafe, in 1972 the Sunday School became a private house, in 1990 the old church was pulled down and a new one erected in 1991.

53 Nrs. 239-247 Gisburn Road. The Fold is just off the picture to the left. It was a common and convenient occurrence to deposit household rubbish into Pendle Water and the deliberate building of the four privies with square outlets testifies to the practice. Not the most hygienic by today's standards and yet it served its purpose. One thought nothing of crossing the road, pushing open the gate, scampering down the steps and past the disturbed hens to sit waiting in the dark seclusion on a winter's night. The subsequent relief was probably reward enough. 239 was occupied in the 1920s to 1940s by Varleys, Sutcliffes and Cooks; 241 by a Mr. and Mrs. Mann – he was a weaver; 243 by Varleys, Kellets, Dugdales, Crooks and Broughtons; 245 by Mr. G. Dunderdale, a weaver, and then Mr. G. Cheesborough, a tram/bus driver; 247 housed Jane Carr the baker, then Taylors, Brierleys and Mr. Loone, the gardener, and his wife.

54 **Urinal corner.** Adjacent to Higherford Mill was the tram terminus, also known as urinal corner for obvious reasons. Prior to 1892 the ancient township of Barrowford was under the control of the Rural Sanitary Authority at Burnley, upon which it had but one representative. The sanitation of the township was said to have been of the most primitive and inefficient character. Whitehall was continually urging upon the R.S.A. the necessity of having the place sewered, but the R.S.A. listened with a tardiness almost approaching point blank refusal. So in 1891 660 ratepayers applied to have formed their own local board. Rates at the time were 2s.1d. in the pound: the poor rate 1s.8d., street lighting 3d., and sanitary 2d. By 1892 Barrowford had obtained the dubious pleasure of being constituted an Urban Sanitary District. By 1960 there were three lavatories and one public convenience situated at strategic points.

55 **Crowtrees Cottage.** This eighteenth century cottage formed part of the Crowtrees Estate that was owned by the Grimshaws, squires of the village in the nineteenth century. Thomas (1765-1842) was the first Grimshaw to live at the larger Crowtrees House, moving there from a house at Higham now known as the Four Alls Inn, in 1805. Thomas and his wife Grace had nine children. Thomas' grandson Thomas (1832-1888) inherted Crowtrees in 1856. His son Thomas Nicholas became town clerk of Wakefield, another son, Charles Edward, became an architect. The Barleydale Road houses were built on part of the Crowtree Estate in 1909. Further building on Barnoldswick Road and Gisburn Road followed the sale of the estate. The Grimshaws ran Higherford Mill, were maltsters and were thoroughly involved with the Higherford Wesleyans. William Henry Atkinson purchased Crowtrees House in 1894 from the trustees of Thomas Grimshaw.

56 Crowtrees House.

William Henry Atkinson was a 25-year old brick maker living at 10 Atkinson Street, Colne, in 1881. In 1891 he had moved to 45 Hagg Street, Colne, as an architect and surveyor with a wife Jane (Greenwood) of Colne. From the mid-1890s Crowtrees was their home and by the time of his death in September 1918 at the age of 63, William had become a successful architect, well known throughout the district where he had a large practice. His wife Jane died in February 1933 aged 77 and one of his daughters, also named Jane, lived at Crowtrees until about 1950. She died at 'Woodlands' Barrowford in 1961 at the age of 74. The large family memorial can be seen in the Inghamite Cemetery at Wheatley Lane. In 1951 Adam MacMurtrie Graham, a consultant obstetrician and gynaecologist at Burnley General Hospital, took up residence with his family. He died in November 1981 and his family left shortly afterwards.

57 The old Higherford Bridge. Three fords once crossed the river at Barrowford: at Newbridge, at Lowerford – where seven roads or tracks led to the crossing opposite the Fleece Inn a little upstream from Victoria Mill –, and at Higherford. Prior to the new Higherford Bridge being built in 1807, the road to Gisburn passed over this Tudor pack horse bridge built about 1583. All the local roads would have been seriously affected by the nineteenth century canal, reservoir and railway developments. All the bridges must have withstood considerable torrents of water that regularly affect and flood the area downstream. Higherford, the earliest of the three fords to be bridged, was built on solid rock and recorded repairs have been purely superficial, the Grimshaw family adding the side walls in the last century. Any further alterations require governmental approval, as in 1927 it was scheduled as an ancient monument.

58 **Barleydale.** An early photograph taken from what is now Barleydale Road shows the old Higherford Bridge; behind it and across the road is the Old Bridge Inn with adjacent farm barn; the buildings right of centre are what was originally Crowtrees House but is now 1 Barleydale Road; those on the extreme right and further back will be Brookdell. Prior to 1915 Barleydale was known as Grimshaw Holme, the houses becoming numbered as well as named from 1952. Barrowford U.D.C. on 17th September 1907 approved the plan submitted by Mr. E. Hart for the erection of fifteen additional houses on the Crowtrees Estate, some of which occupy the farm meadow in the foreground of the photograph. The Catholic church built in 1898 now obstructs the view beyond the bridge, on the left of which are hidden the five houses of Rockville that were erected by Hartley Ashworth in the late 1870s and were then known as Rock Villas.

59 **The Old Oak Tea Garden.** A lot of folks will remember being taken on the path towards Grimshaw's oak. There was a tennis club (Holme Lea) and you could get jugs and pots of tea from Sharps wood hut. Their daughter Nell was going to be a pianist and she practised upstairs in the hut. However, a polyp in her nose went the wrong way and killed her whilst only in her teens. She was a lovely girl, very bonny. Her father and mother never got over the tragedy. The shop used to make lovely ice cream and on the front wall of the tea room was an electric shock machine, one penny in the slot, clutch the brass knob, slide the handle and hold tight. Mrs. Sharp, the owner, is shown standing outside. When in August 1923 Barrowford Council decided to serve a notice on the owner and occupier to remove the wooden structure now being used as a shop and dwelling house, there was some doubt as to whether a plan for the building had ever been approved.

60 **The Grimshaw Oak.** Half a mile up the river from Higherford Bridge and past Barleydale Road you can walk beside the water flow until you come to a little black and white cottage on the left. Standing to its left is one of the few remaining denizens of a forest long gone and known as the Grimshaw Oak after a major local landowning family. Its limbs are dismembered, its bark is not securely attached overall and its continued existence seems suspect. Veevers in 1892 wrote that 'a tale hangs from every outstretched branch … and mid countless changes this has nobly stood, resisting all the force of storm or flood'. Fielding suggested in 1905 that it had flourished for seven or eight hundred years and gave its girth as sixteen feet ten inches. Blakey in 1929 gave its girth as eighteen feet, and today (1997) measured four feet above ground level its girth is eighteen feet nine inches.

61 Watermeetings farm about 1920. The pathway along the stream side and up to what is now Blacko post office was once a favourite Sunday walk when you wore the best clothes. Watermeetings farm was probably built in the third quarter of the 17th century with the Sharp family living there for over 130 years. John came from Scotland, his wife Ellen from Whitehough, where she was born in 1777. They had five children and one of them, Mark, had a further 13 children. The Sharps had a market garden and Rose Sharp used to sit outside the farm selling raspberries and strawberries that she had grown. They were sold in wicker baskets twelve inches high. Rose died in 1931 aged 84. Wilfred Sharp (born in 1882) invented a special farm tractor and a gun whose patent was taken up by the War Office. Another Sharp had a cloggers' shop near Barrowford post office. Kenneth Sharp was headmaster of Barrowford school in the 1950s.

62 Utherstone valley about 1912. This Pendle Water is one of the main headwaters of the river Calder. Arising partly on the southern dip slopes of Pendle Hill and partly north of Barley, it cuts its way through the Pendle Grit at Barley, then crosses the Warley Wise Grit near Whitehough and cuts through the Kinderscout and upper beds of the Millstone Grit near Higherford. Pendle Water is joined by Colne Water at Reedyford, joins the Calder north of Burnley and the river Ribble west of Whalley. Boulder clay is the most widespread of glacial remains and drift deposits are a feature of the valleys between Barley, Roughlee and Blacko. The almost total absence of rock exposures along large lengths of the river suggests a thickness of boulder clay greater than 20 feet. Downstream from Watermeetings the river seems engaged in cleaning out the old pre-glacial valley to the underlying Noggarth Grit, seen at the old Higherford Bridge.

63 Utherstone Wood. In 1892 Barrowford Local Board was formed and two years later, in 1894, by the Local Government Board order number 31617, two new townships were created: Barrowford, the urban council district; and Blacko, the rural portion to the north. Blacko parish had 997 acres including one acre of inland water, a population of 300, 113 electors, and P. Haythornthwaite, J. Metcalfe, J. Trafford, T. Moore and W. Standing as councillors. A very pretty area of Blacko is Utherstone, sometimes spelt Otherstone, where Blacko Water and Pendle Water meet. J. Widdup suggests that Utherstone (pronounced utherstan) is probably a corruption of heather stone. The name Blacko means black hill, being based on the Norse word for a hill, haugr. The height of Blacko hill is 1,018 feet above sea level, the river area in the photograph being in the region of 475 feet above sea level.

View at Utherstone, Near Barrowford.

64 **Watermeetings.** An idyllic scene in good weather but a source of floods on many an occasion as a result of the enormous amounts of water brought together at this spot and channelled with an added fury towards the apprehensive residents of Barrowford a mile down river. Early records exist for great quantities of water being discharged from Pendle Hill in 1580 and 1669, and for a Betty Harris being blown into the river and drowned in 1787. In 1837 the Barrowford to Nelson bridge was washed away; in about 1840 a youth named Ridehalgh was washed away, his body never recovered; there was a great flood in 1866; in 1879 a man named Bracewell with horse and trap got into difficulties at Roughlee waterfall, he and the trap parting company there. His body was washed all through Barrowford and recovered at Walverden Water. In 1880 pig and poultry keepers had to wade in up to their waists to rescue stranded stock.

65 **The Grange.** Built in 1841 at the junction of the roads to Gisburn and Barnoldswick, The Grange passed between several members of the Grimshaw family before being purchased in 1870 for £1,000 by John Holroyd and Sagar Brown, both of Colne. In 1871 it was sold for £1,585 to a maltster Nicholas Strickland, passing to his son John later. At an auction sale at the Nelson Inn in 1899 it was offered as having two cellars; a dining room 15' x 15', a drawing room 18' x 15', scullery, pantry, five bedrooms, bathroom, W.C.; stable, coach house and hay lofts. Thomas Percy Smith, an electrical engineer, vacated The Grange for Netherheys in 1911 when John Dixon, a cotton manufacturer of Holmfield Mill, took over. Rex Mayall was there from the 1930s until 1960, the Halsteads in the 1960s and from the early 1970s the owner has been Ronald Cleveland Foster (formerly of Cleveland Guest) and well known for his many public services.

66 **Hospital effort at The Grange.** Pictured at the opening ceremony are, from left to right: Mr. Armistead, clerk to Barrowford U.D.C.; James Holden, Samuel Holden, Richard Holden, brother of James; E. Jackson and John Trafford, the opener who was a manufacturer at Blacko. Mr. Armistead was organist at Reedyford Wesleyan chapel, lived at Parkhill until his death in 1967 and his widow until her death in 1973 aged 92. James Holden was a gentleman farmer and cotton manufacturer. He had three daughters, Eleanor, Elizabeth and Mary. Samuel Holden (Holmfield Mill) lived at Blacko; his son was killed in the First World War and his name is on Blacko cenotaph; his daughter Beatrice became Mrs. Hindley – a chairman of Barrowford Council; his daughter Gladys never married; his daughter Madge married Rex Mayall, an Armenian who became a director in the mill. The latter lived at The Grange, Madge writing a book on her travels in East Africa.

67 **Blacko village.** Formerly a portion of the township of Barrowford, Blacko became a separate parish under the Local Government Act of 1894. The principal landowners of its 997 acres were the executors of James Grimshaw Esq., J. Hall Esq., and John Holt Esq. Its allegiances were varied, being in the parliamentary division of Clitheroe but in the county council division of Barrowford. Its population was in 1891: 400; 1901: 485; 1911: 502; 1921: 550; 1931: 551; 1951: 463; 1961: 453; 1971: 450; 1981: 514; 1991: 573. The photograph shows Blacko before the tower was built on the background hill in 1890. Blacko (the black hill) is 1,018 feet high. Other local hills are as follows: Boulsworth (bull's neck) 1,700 ft; Noyna (noon hill) 980 ft; Pendle (head hill) 1,831 ft; Pike Law (pointed hill) 1,189 ft; Stank Top (pole top) 1,060 ft. From all of them there are magnificent views of the surrounding countryside.

68 **Below the Rising Sun.**
The plain sided building on the left of the picture is the Rising Sun inn and below from left to right are the cottages now numbered 324 to 310, that were 20 to 4 Gisburn Road, Blacko, prior to 1969. 20 was for many years the house of Thomas Brown (died in 1948), market gardener for fifty years and chairman of Blacko parish council for twenty years; 18 in the early 1900s was the post office; 16 from 1933 to 1960 held a Mr. Walton who died at 87; Giambetta Berry the weaver lived at 12 from 1923 until his death in 1944; John Cook of 10 said there was a herb to cure every illness and never had a doctor from being born until just before his death on Easter Sunday 1928, the same day as his wife had died three years earlier; James Bond the clothlooker lived at 8 – inseparable from his dog; he had a never failing fund of jokes and is remembered by children of that date as a marvellous kite maker, until his death in 1935.

69 **Cottages full of characters.** The row of cottages on the left is now numbered 441 to 453, but before 1969 they were numbered from 3 to 15. The Co-op was at Blacko in 1893 as the Barrowford Progressive Co-operative Society. From the 1930s at least it was at 3 Gisburn Road as a branch of Nelson Co-op, and in October 1966 it had become a private house for Mr. and Mrs. Mather. Chippendale Walton, the market gardener, lived at 5 in the early 1900s and in the 1930s and 1940s John Wick, the produce merchant and carrier, was there. Mendelssohn Bannister lived at 7 in 1941 and Handel Whitehead next door at 9 in the 1920s and 1930s. John Hargreaves, the oat cake baker, lived at 15 from about 1905 until the mid-1920s. He was severely handicapped, having lost a leg at the age of 8. For many years he worked as a twister at Springfield Mill. Nevertheless he was a keen cyclist and enjoyed swimming, particularly in the Lake District. He died in 1941 in his 77th year.

70 **Upper Brow, Blacko, 1902.** I wonder who he was and what he could tell us about the events in his developing village. About the Board School behind him with John Clegg in charge of the mixed department and Miss Minnie Brown in charge of the infants. The parish council at that time included a Hartley Broughton, who lived at 62 (now 396) Gisburn Road – a house behind the centre tree. He was a healthy man, his only ailment being a dose of flu for which he had a bottle of medicine in February 1929, but in December 1929 he was found dead in his hen pen, 64 years old. His son and daughter in law Bessie also lived at 62. She had worked for her father in law's nursery since getting married about 1921, and also in the Nelson shop at Manchester Road from about 1936. She died in 1971 and like Hartley Broughton and many other Blacko folk was buried at Wheatley Lane Inghamite Church. Jonathan Henderson of 64 (398) was the newsagent – a real character.

71 **John Clegg and Blacko School.** John Clegg, on the left of the picture, replaced a Mr. Hindle as headmaster in December 1882. He retired $38^1/_2$ years later on 31st July 1921, recording in the school log book: 'The scholars, teachers, parents, old scholars, managers and friends presented me with a beautiful wallet and £50. Mrs. Clegg received a pair of silver candlesticks and a bouquet of flowers. A committee of the inhabitants of Blacko and teachers, made all arrangements and organised a field day with sports for the children and adults. Buns and coffee were served on the field. The whole proceedings went very satisfactorily, a suitable finish to one's life work at Blacko School.' Mr. Clegg is remembered as a gentleman to whom children could talk at any time. He would take groups of children up Pendle Hill and buy them pop at the Barley Post Office. On the right of the picture is Mrs. Eastwood.

72 **Blacko Chapel.** The group of Wesleyan Reformers and Free Gospellers who held their services in a cottage at Browbottom and their 'annual sermons' in a barn at Spouthouses or in the weaving shed, formed a building committee in 1865, appointed John Landless of Colne as architect and proceeded to build the Ebenezer Chapel. The foundation stone was laid in 1867 and further stones for the builders were delivered free of charge by local farmers. The chapel was opened in 1868 with a debt of £600, subsequent developments being the installation of a new organ in 1889, the earliest use in the area of a 49 foot ladder for pointing repairs and the collapse of a 30 foot roof timber in 1951 with a repair bill of £1,000 for the average congregation of 30. An interesting custom was that after a village marriage the bride, bridegroom and attendants would all come to chapel the following Sunday dressed in their wedding attire.

73　**War memorial.** Brownley Park Farm in background. The war memorial was unveiled in May 1921. Of those recorded there Rufus Brown, an RAMC stretcher bearer aged 29, was captured and died in hospital. At Blacko he had been an assistant organist and choirmaster. Septimus Nicholson's mate Cpl. Rogers 'couldn't get to him before he was gone' but wrote to the ex-weaver's wife and child at 54 Gisburn Road expressing deepest sympathy. 2nd. Lieut. Ernest Airlie Holden was 23 years old when he died in 1916, having had both legs amputated below the knee. He had been a salesman for Holden Bros. at Barrowford. Alfred B. Moorhouse, a Sunday School teacher and articled accountant, joined the army when only 19. A shell explosion killed him a year later. On any advance he had always been first over the top and his obituary suggests that 'the comforting fact abides that Pte. Moorhouse has not lived … and died in vain'. I wonder.

74 **Gisburn Road, Blacko.**

The houses on the left, now 440 to 460, were numbered 76 to 94 prior to 1969, with 440 being the same as Braeside. The opposite side similarly had a change, 527 to 561 being 21a to 53. Below the left-hand side houses is the Methodist Chapel, below the right is Springfield Mill, that employed many of the local residents under its various owners, the Traffords of Braeside being there from 1905 to 1938. Richard Nutter of 37 was a weaver there. Born at Cockhill Farm in Colne he died in 1941 aged 71. Luke Berry of 84 and 87 was a tackler when the mill belonged to Hartleys. He died in 1934 aged 88. Isaiah Tattersall of 82 worked there as did Richard (Dickie) Jay of 47, who like his father was an engine tenter. Dickie and his wife Mary, who came from Malkin Tower farm, had a quiet golden wedding in 1955, but got a 12 lb. wedding cake to celebrate the occasion. Every house can tell you its own fascinating story.

75 **Blacko Tower.** Built originally by Jonathan Stansfield, a hardworking, enterprising man who ran a grocery store in David Street founded by his father in 1820, the tower was 30 feet high with a diameter of 12 feet. The stone came from the other side of the hill and masons worked under Jonathan's direction from 1882 until 1890. One of the early ideas was to provide afternoon teas and serve them on top of the tower. Jonathan died in 1894 aged 71. In 1948 the top part of the tower had collapsed, only one castellation remaining and the flooring of the gallery had completely gone. It was in a dangerous state, so Frank Barritt of Colne instigated repair and restoration work enlisting the aid of the scouts of Colne and district. Further restoration work took place in 1971 – mainly around the doorway – with encouragement from Miss Hilda Fort, headmistress, and the children of Blacko Primary School.

76 Hollin Hall, Blacko.

Hollin, meaning holly, is a name frequently found in this area with examples in Colne, Trawden, Foulridge, Brierfield and Blacko. Hollin Hall in the picture is on Barnoldswick Road at Blacko. The cottages have been occupied certainly from the mid-1800s. In 1841 one house had George Wood (60) a cotton weaver, Nancy (20) and George (21); another had John Rushton (40), Martha (40), Mary (15), Sarah (9), all cotton weavers, and Ann (5); another had Ellis Stansfield (30), Elizabeth (30), Mary (8), weavers, and Thomas (2); in another was Isabella (35) and John Fowler (10), both cotton weavers, together with John Parker (50), Mary (25), Martha (25), all weavers, and Ann (1) and Elizabeth (7 months) – a full house. Subsequent census records show a similar preponderance of weavers. Now named New Houses, the two centre ones have been combined and sit snugly behind a new wooden sign displaying 'Hollin Hall'.